# ROUGH AND READY
# COWBOYS

## A. S. GINTZLER

JOHN MUIR PUBLICATIONS
SANTA FE, NEW MEXICO

# Acknowledgments

To the cowboys and their chroniclers.

John Muir Publications, P.O. Box 613, Santa Fe, New Mexico 87504
© 1994 by John Muir Publications
Printed in the United States of America

First edition. First printing March 1994
First TWG printing March 1994

Library of Congress Cataloging-in-Publication Data
Gintzler, A. S.
Rough and ready cowboys  /  A. S. Gintzler
p.    cm.
Includes index.
ISBN 1-56261-152-6  :  $12.95
1. Cowboys—West (U.S.)—History—19th century—Juvenile literature.  2.  West (U.S.)—Social life and customs—Juvenile literature. [1.  Cowboys.  2.  West(U.S.)—Social life and customs.] I. Title.
F596.G57  1994
978'.02—dc20                          93-32343
                                      CIP
                                      AC

Logo Design: Chris Brigman
Interior Design and Typography: Linda Braun
Illustrations: Chris Brigman
Printer: Arcata Graphics/Kingsport

Distributed to the book trade by
W. W. Norton & Co., Inc.
500 Fifth Avenue
New York, NY 10110

Distributed to the education market by
The Wright Group
19201 120th Avenue N.E.
Bothell, WA 98011-9512

Cover photo, cowboys gather around the
   chuck wagon © The Bettmann Archive
Back cover photo, cowboy on a horse, 1887
   © The Bettman Archive
Title page photo, New Mexico cowboys, around 1900 © Museum of New Mexico

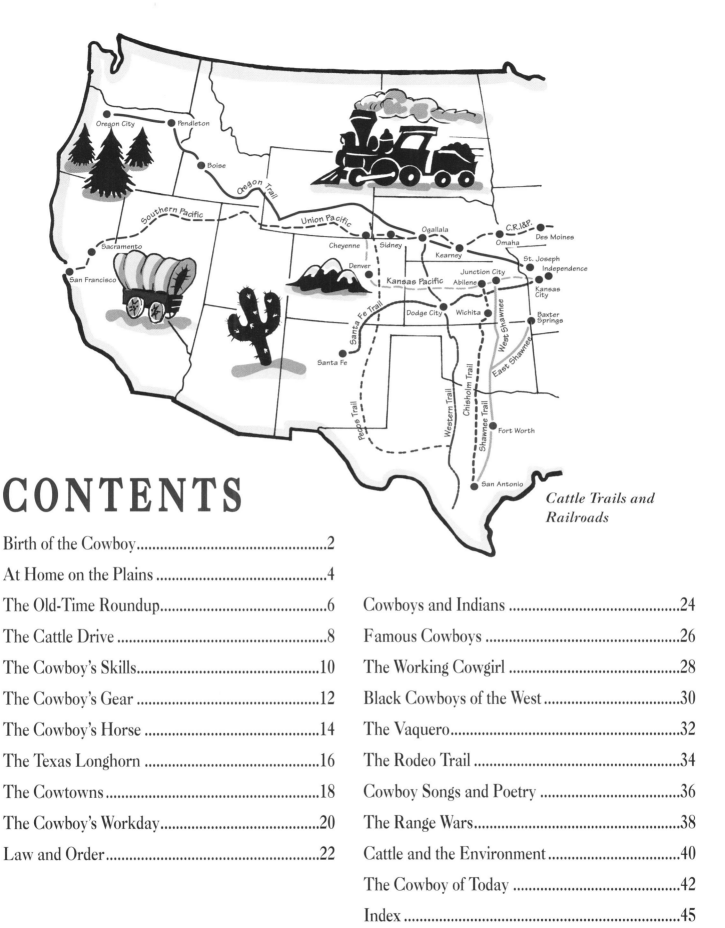

*Cattle Trails and Railroads*

# CONTENTS

# Birth of the Cowboy

The earliest cowboys boasted that they were born "half horse and half alligator." But they weren't born in Texas—not at first. Bands of revolutionaries and British loyalists called "cow-boys" rustled cattle from each other in the 1700s during the American Revolution. After the war these eastern cowboys drifted west. Many became hands on river boats and rode the Mississippi River south—like alligators—down to New Orleans. In the early 1800s they drifted west into the Texas frontier.

In those days, Texas was still part of Mexico, and the land was teeming with wild cattle and horses. Mexican cowboys, called *vaqueros* (vah-KAY-rohs), had been herding cattle on horseback for generations. They wore wide-brimmed hats called *sombreros* (sahm-BRAY-rohs) and caught cattle with a rope called *la reata* (lah ree-AH-tah). It was from the Mexican vaquero that the Texas cowboy borrowed his tools of the trade—and his cows.

The Bettmann Archive

*Cowboys sometimes had time to horse around*

In 1835, the citizens of Texas won their own war of independence against Mexico and became the Republic of Texas. The Mexican ranchers were forced out, and the Texas cowboys claimed their herds of cattle. As the eastern cowboy came West and learned to rope cattle and ride mustangs, the vaquero's *la reata* became the cowboy's "lariat." But how did the horses and cows get to Texas in the first place?

There were no horses or cows in North America or South America until Columbus arrived. He brought Spanish horses and cattle on his second voyage to the Americas. Some of the cattle and horses got free and found abundant food on the prairies of South America. Soon wild herds spread throughout the continent. Later, horsemen hunted and slaughtered these wild cattle on the plains of Argentina and Brazil. These were really the first cowboys—250 years before America's Revolutionary War.

## HUASOS, GAUCHOS, AND LLANEROS

The *huaso* (HWAH-soh) of Chile and the *llanero* (yahn-AY-roh) of Venezuela were the first cowboys. In Argentina, cowboys called *gauchos* (GOW-chohs) became national heroes. They rode the broad plains as ranch hands working for low wages. Gauchos were fiercely independent men who needed little more than a horse, a lasso, and a knife to survive.

*Gauchos on a ranch in Argentina*

In 1519, the Spanish explorer Cortés brought the first horses into Mexico. Other expeditions brought cattle. By the 1600s, huge herds of wild horses and cattle roamed the plains of Mexico and up into Texas. Native peoples, whom Columbus called "Indians," learned to ride and hunt wild cows in Mexico from the Spanish invaders. A new race of mixed-blood people was born from the union of Spanish and native peoples—the *mestizos* (meh-STEE-zohs). Most of the vaqueros of Mexico and Texas were mestizos.

The American cowboy didn't really find fame until after the Civil War. In the late 1860s, the first big Texas cattle drives herded cattle north to the new railroads in Kansas. The railroads made it possible to ship cattle quickly to slaugherhouses and markets back East.

Cows quickly became big business. The West became cattle country, with a new breed of cowboy driving herds on the open range from Texas to Canada. These cowboys were descendants of the eastern cowboys who fought in the Revolutionary War. Some were freed African American slaves who brought their hopes west. Others were Mexican American vaqueros who developed the skills and passed them on.

Cowboys were a new breed of laborer—"half horse and half alligator"—working on the American frontier.

*The American cowboy borrowed the tools of his trade from the Mexican vaquero*

3

# At Home on the Plains

The cowboy's home was a huge stretch of land smack in the middle of North America. Back East, people called it the "Great American Desert." Today, it's better known as the Great Plains. The Plains stretch from Texas to Canada and from Missouri to the Rocky Mountains.

The land was wild with buffalo and antelope, grizzly bears, wolves, and bobcats. A person could get lost there and never be found. Water was scarce. The cowboys, however, made these rugged windswept plains their home.

The Spanish *conquistador* (cohn-KEES-tah-dohr) Francisco Coronado was the first European to enter the Great Plains. In 1541, he traveled there from Mexico looking for gold. He didn't find any. Instead he found miles of grasslands cut by rivers and dry ravines.

Another Spanish conquistador named Hernán Cortés also traveled through the Great Plains. There, he found Native American farmers and hunters living in tribal villages. They grew corn and hunted buffalo and deer on foot. They'd never seen men on horses before. But they were soon riding and hunting on horseback. By 1680, the native tribes had driven the Spanish back down to Mexico—and kept their horses. Horses gave the Pawnee, Sioux, Cheyenne, and other tribes mastery of the Plains.

*The Great Plains*

In the 1700s, English and French explorers and trappers began trading guns and hides with Plains tribes. Life on the Plains was changing. By the mid-1800s, other white men were crossing the Plains on their way to California in search of gold, or to Oregon's rich farmland. But they didn't care to linger. Few were interested in stopping in the middle of 2,000 miles of flat, dry prairie.

## THE RANGE OF THE BUFFALO

Huge herds of buffalo ranged the Great Plains for 2,000 years before the cowboy arrived. Around 1860, some 50 million buffalo, also called bison, roamed trails from Mexico to Canada. But by 1887, fewer than 1,000 buffalo remained. White men such as Buffalo Bill Cody slaughtered the herds for their hides and for meat to feed railroad building crews, or just to make room for cattle. Today, more than 100,000 buffalo live in protected herds in North America.

*Cheyenne chiefs, around 1890*

The Native Americans continued to hunt the vast herds of migrating buffalo that fed on plains grasses. Once the Indians had horses, they quickly became excellent riders and horse trainers. For people who could live in the wild on horseback and for animals who could graze the grasses, the Plains were a land of plenty.

At the southern end of the Plains, Texas cowboys were hunting and herding wild cattle as early as the 1820s. These cows had come up out of Mexico and spread into Texas. When the railroad was extended from the East into Missouri and Kansas in 1865, the Texas cowboys began herding the cattle north to railroad towns.

Year after year, cowboys drove thousands of cattle across the dry and dusty Great Plains. And they didn't move in a hurry. Cattle can't be rushed, so the cowboy took his time. The land shaped him during these long months on the trail. Wide open spaces, endless sky, encounters with Indians, buffalo stampedes, and strange wildlife challenged his endurance. Not every cowboy survived. Those who did adapted to the Plains and adopted the grassland and the desert as their home. From Texas to Montana, the cowboy became as common a sight as the Indian he often fought.

*A roundup on the wide, open plains*

# The Old-Time Roundup

The first roundups in Texas began in the mid-1800s. In those days, there were no fences to contain the cattle. Cattle roamed freely over the open range. During the Civil War, herds in Texas ran wild, so cattlemen returning from the war had to hunt up lost cows. Violent disagreements broke out over cattle and range lands.

Finally, the Texas ranchers borrowed the roundup system—the *rodeo* (roh-DAY-oh)—that Mexican ranchers had developed. Early rodeos in Mexico weren't public events—they were roundups to gather and separate herds. The roundup system spread from Mexico north to Canada. Range lands were divided into districts. The cattlemen from each district appointed a roundup judge, hired cowboys, and gathered equipment. This took weeks of planning.

*Cowboys whooping it up*

Twice a year, cowboys had to round up cattle on the open range. Spring roundup, usually in May, was the beginning of the cowboy's work year. At this time, cowboys gathered untended herds that had drifted during the winter and branded calves. After branding, cattle were turned loose on the open range to graze.

In the early fall, when the cattle had fattened up on plains grasses, they were rounded up again. This time, cowboys separated the cows that would be driven to market. Those bound for the slaughterhouse were usually the older cows and steers, which are male cows unable to breed. Younger cows and bulls remained on the range as "breeding stock" to increase the herd.

For every roundup, each rancher supplied cowboys, a supervisor, a herd of horses called a *remuda* (ray-MOO-dah), and a wagon of "chuck"—slang for food. Over several days, they gathered at a central point on a range district.

When all had arrived—as many as three hundred cowboys!—the work began. A wrangler roped a string of horses from the remuda for each cowboy. After a breakfast of coffee, beef, and biscuits, cowboys saddled their mounts and rode out.

They traveled in a double column to the first section of range, then spread out in pairs. The pairs herded cattle to a "bunch ground," a central area where they were kept from straying. By noon, the cowboys had rounded up a thousand or more cows. The roundup captain posted two of the men to watch the herd. The rest broke for lunch and to saddle up fresh horses.

The toughest work came next. Several cowboys on "cutting" horses rode through the herd separating cattle by brand, the symbol of the ranch that owned them. Then cowboys on horseback lassoed the calves, brought them down, and branded them with red-hot irons. By day's end, worn out cowboys wolfed down their chuck at the new camp and rolled out their blankets. They slept in shifts. Pairs of cowboys rode night guard circling the herds, changing guard every two hours.

*A cowboy lassos a cow*

Each day for thirty days, the camp moved to another section of range and rounded up more cattle. After the roundup, cowboys competed in bronco riding, roping, and other skills, before moving on.

### RED HOT BRANDS

Brands are symbols burnt into a calf's flesh with red hot irons to identify the owner. In a herd, calves stay very close to their mothers. A cowboy would rope a calf and call out its mother's brand to the cowboy tending the branding fire. Then he would drag the calf to the branding spot, where it was pulled to the ground and branded. When it was released, it would scurry back to its mother.

*Types of brands*

# The Cattle Drive

The great cattle drives to railroad towns in Kansas began around 1867 and continued for the next twenty years. They were the cowboy's best and busiest years. But the first drives on trails out of Texas began in the 1850s. Around 1849, gold was discovered in California, and Americans headed west in droves. California quickly became a big market for beef. Texas cowboys drove cattle west on the California Trail to San Francisco. Cowboys could buy longhorns in Texas for $10 and sell them in California for $100 each, but they lost many along the way. Other Texans drove longhorns to markets back East. Trails such as the Osage Trace, Kansas, and Shawnee passed through Indian lands before reaching the early railroad stations in Ohio. To make big profits faster, however, the cattlemen needed stations closer to Texas. A rail line to Abilene, Kansas, opened in 1867. From there, cattle could be sent in boxcars to slaughterhouses in Chicago. This was the beginning of the great cattle drives along the Chisholm Trail that made American cowboys famous around the world.

Soon other trails became established, like the Western Trail to Dodge City, the Bozeman Trail to Montana, and the Goodnight-Loving Trail to Colorado and Wyoming.

Texas ranchers hired professional organizers, called "drovers," to round up and deliver their livestock to market. The drover would hire a trail boss and a dozen or so cowboys.

Museum of New Mexico

*Cattle moving through an arroyo*

The Bettmann Archive

*The night watch*

In the early days, range cowboys cooked for themselves. But on the big drives, the drovers were responsible for cooking "chuck." The chuck wagon was a simple lumber wagon converted to a pantry on wheels. A cook prepared stews over open fire pits and baked fresh biscuits in portable ovens. Flour, beans, and bacon were typical chuck. The cook made stick-to-your-ribs meals like "son-of-a-gun stew" and "sucama-growl," a sweet dumpling.

*A chuck break*

Museum of New Mexico

He also purchased a remuda, about 120 horses that would be used by the cowboys on the three-month drive north. Each cowboy chose a string of ten horses from the remuda, because he had to change mounts frequently to rest them. All the cowboy needed of his own was a saddle, a rope, and his clothes.

The herd moved like a long snake through canyons and across rivers. In the lead was the trail boss who scouted ahead for water and river crossings. Off to the left, a horse wrangler guided the remuda. Two cowboys rode "point" on either side of the lead cows. Further back were two "swing" riders and behind them were two more at "flank." The youngest and least skilled cowboys got the dustiest job—riding "drag" behind the herd to keep the slowest cows moving. At the end of the day, the herd would be brought together to bed down.

Bad weather, rough terrain, and rushing rivers made for slow progress up the trails. It took very little to stampede a herd of cattle, but it took days to pull the herd back together. Severe drought and the dust storms that followed could blind an entire herd. Cattle thieves, called rustlers, often ambushed cowboys, driving off and stealing the cattle. Cowboys slept in shifts so that several of them were always slowly circling the herd. If they didn't lose the herds or their own lives, cowboys got paid at trail's end. There they blew off steam, spent their money, then headed back to Texas for the next drive north.

# The Cowboy's Skills

The old-time cowboy had to be a jack-of-all-trades. Riding, roping, and branding were just a few of his skills. He also did blacksmithing, cow and horse doctoring, and leather tooling.

Roping was more than just throwing a lasso over a cow's head. A cowboy had to be able to rope a cow or a horse while on foot or horseback. He had to know several roping techniques—the head catch, forefooting, and heeling—and he had to be good at all of them. Even one technique, like the head catch—throwing the loop over an animal's head—required different types of throws. A cowboy on horseback most often used an overhanded throw to rope a cow. Underhanded throws could be used from horseback or on the ground. When in a corral, a cowboy rarely whirled his rope overhead because it made the cattle nervous.

*The Bettmann Archive*

*Throwing the lasso*

In the early 1800s and before, cowboys had to make their own ropes from rawhide or plant fibers. They learned the skill of braiding rawhide, horsehair, and hemp from Mexican vaqueros. Ropes, whips, halters, bridles, and other cowboy tools were all handmade.

## CATCHING A MUSTANG

The early cowboys caught individual wild horses, called mustangs, with ropes. Later, they thought of ways to catch large numbers of them. Dead-end, or box canyons were great traps. After finding a wild herd, cowboys built a strong fence with a large gate across the open end of the canyon. Then they spread out and chased the mustangs into the canyon and through the gate. Once inside the fence, the gate was slammed behind them.

*Heading into the box canyon*

After manufactured rope became available, cowboys still had to protect and soften their ropes and leather gear with tallow, or melted animal fat, and wax.

There was more to riding than just staying on a horse. A good cowboy knew how to capture wild horses, "break" them, and train them to work a herd. It took years of training and patience to "educate" a good cutting or roping horse. Not every horse had the reflexes and the "smarts" to cut a cow from a herd. And not every cowboy had the skill and talent to train horses.

Moving cattle up a trail called for a mixture of riding ability, good "cow sense," and toughness. A good cowboy had all of these. He could ride "point" and bend the herd by riding at precise angles and then dropping back at the right moment. A good point man could read the land and carefully drive cattle through dangerous rivers and boggy creeks.

On the open range, there were no blacksmiths or veterinarians nearby. Range cowboys shoed their own horses and tended their injuries. Open wounds in an animal's flesh would fester with maggots and kill the animal if left untreated. Cowboys cleaned these wounds with chloroform and dressed them with cow dung. They saved many cows and horses with these simple remedies.

*Busting a bronco*

The Bettmann Archive

The range cowboy was also skilled in the use of a "running iron." These were light, versatile branding irons with a curve at one end. Unlike a regular branding iron, a running iron could be used to draw any brand needed on a cow's hide. This was the favorite tool of the cattle rustler. He used it to change the look of brands so that ranchers could not identify their cows.

# The Cowboy's Gear

The cowboy was outfitted for work from head to toe. Much of his gear was developed by the South American cowboy and came north with the vaquero. The cowboy's lariat and chaps were direct copies of the vaquero's *la reata* and *chaparejos* (shah-pah-RAY-hose). His high-crowned hat was modeled on the vaquero's sombrero. Over the years, the gear changed with the times, working conditions, materials, and needs of the open range cowboy.

The wide-brimmed sombrero of the Southwest protected the cowboy from the scorching sun. The high-crowned Montana hat had carefully placed folds to drain runoff from heavy rains. The cowboy sometimes used his hat to scoop water or to fan a fire.

A cowboy's boots were designed for life in the saddle. The high tops protected his shins and kept sand and grit out. The narrow toes made it easy to quickly slip a boot into a stirrup. The high heels kept the boot from slipping all the way through. A cowboy's greatest fear was to get his foot caught in a stirrup when his horse fell or became frightened and threw him off.

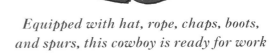

*Equipped with hat, rope, chaps, boots, and spurs, this cowboy is ready for work*

*A good cowboy blunted the sharp points of his spurs*

The spurs on his boots were used to get his horse's attention in tight spots. A good cowboy would blunt the spur points, called rowels, with a file. A cowboy who hurt a horse with his spurs was soon out of a job.

Bridles, lariats, and riding whips were braided by hand from rawhide strips, horse hair, or hemp. The earliest vaquero ropes were 30 to 35 feet of braided rawhide. When the vaquero came north, he also brought a fiber rope made from the maguey plant. But rope material and length varied with the climate. In the dry Southwest, maguey ropes worked best. In the damp Northwest, however, these ropes became too stiff. Ropes as long as 60 feet were used to rope cattle on the open range. Shorter ropes were used for work in the corral.

## SADDLE 'EM UP

The first saddles used in the Americas were brought by Spanish *conquistadores*. Designed for use in battle, the seat of this saddle wrapped completely around the rider. The vaqueros made the saddle smaller and added a "horn" to the front. This horn served as an anchor in the roping technique called "dallying." The early Texas saddles were held on by two straps, called cinches. Most modern western saddles have only one cinch.

*A Texas saddle*

The Bettmann Archive

Bridles with reins were used to control and guide the horse. Most vaqueros trained and rode horses with "hackamore" bridles that slipped around the horse's nose like a noose. The Plains cowboys usually preferred bridles with thin metal bars, called bits, that passed through the horse's mouth. When the reins are pulled on a bit bridle, the bit digs into the flesh of the horse's mouth. Indians seldom used bit bridles on their horses.

The cowboy's bedroll consisted of a waterproof tarp and several blankets and quilts. He called it his "flea trap." In the morning, he rolled his loose belongings into his bedroll and stored it in the supply wagon.

Chaps were made of tough cowhide and strapped over the front of a cowboy's legs. They provided great protection when riding through mesquite thickets and thorny brush. In heavy rains, a cowboy's slicker or raincoat kept him dry. Every part of the cowboy's gear helped him do his job. And most of what he used, he made himself.

*The most important part of a cowboy's gear was his horse. This horse is wearing a bit bridle.*

The Bettmann Archive

# The Cowboy's Horse

The cowboy lived to ride and hated the very idea of walking on his own two feet. A good horse was a cowboy's greatest asset. A bad horse could kill him.

In prehistoric times, herds of wild horses roamed the American plains, but they eventually died off.

*Wild horses often bucked until they got used to the saddle*

Early cowboys throughout the Americas captured and tamed a new breed of wild horse known as mustangs. Mustangs were descended from the Spanish horses brought by Columbus and other Spanish explorers.

Mustangs were soon multiplying in the wild. Indians caught them and became expert trainers and riders. Cheyenne and Sioux on the northern plains learned to hunt buffalo on horseback. Apaches and Comanches became mounted warriors in their efforts to keep the white man out of their home-lands. As the wild and cap-tured herds of horses grew, the American plains were changed forever. Mustangs were small, but tough. They weighed about 600 pounds. Most had reddish-brown coats, sometimes sprin-kled with white. Indians often bred spotted pintos. However, the real measure of a horse wasn't its color, but its performance.

*New Mexico cowboys, around 1900*

A bronco, or wild horse, had to be "broken," or tamed, before it could be ridden and trained. Horses that were bullied and beaten into submission could never be trusted. Horses treated kindly and firmly were more easily trained. Nearly every horse bucked wildly when a saddle was first put on it. But after it got used to the saddle, the horse usually let itself be mounted without bucking the rider. A cowboy who specialized in "bustin' broncs" was called a "bronc breaker," "bronc snapper," or "bronc twister."

On a roundup or on the trail, each cowboy had a string of eight to ten horses for his own use. A horse with a big round belly might be a good "swimmer" for crossing rivers. A good "night" horse knew how to avoid prairie dog holes in the dark. A good "roper" kept a tight rope on a lassoed cow, even after the cowboy dismounted. A prized "cutting" horse could "cut," or separate, a steer from the herd. A smart, well-trained cow horse knew exactly what to do with little or no urging from the cowboy. But a poorly broken horse could be ornery. Cowboys called such horses "spoiled" and avoided riding them.

Mustangs were a hardy breed adapted to survive in the wild. They were sure-footed and quick-witted. To create bigger and stronger mounts, ranchers bred their mustangs with larger horses from the East that had originally come from other parts of the world. These new breeds weighed around 800 pounds and had gentler natures.

A cowboy took pride in his horses even though he didn't own them. They belonged to the rancher's remuda. An experienced cowboy was a good judge of "horseflesh" and had first pick of his string of horses. A young, inexperienced cowboy, or "tenderfoot," had last pick of the leftover "plugs" and "shad-bellies." He didn't need much better when riding "drag" behind the herd.

## HORSESHOEING

A working horse that runs hard through rocky terrain can easily break its hooves and become lame. That's why cowboys nail iron horseshoes to the bottom of their horse's hooves. A blacksmith can exactly fit iron shoes to a horse's hooves by heating the shoes red hot in fire and then pounding them with hammers to the exact shape needed. On the open range, a skilled cowboy can "cold shoe" a horse that loses a shoe by shaping a new one with a file.

*"Cold shoeing" a horse*

# The Texas Longhorn

The first cows in North America tramped onto the Plains with Coronado, the Spanish conquistador. He herded the black, yellow, white, and mottled cows north from Mexico into the area that is now the southwest United States. These cows were of Andalusian stock, named for a region in southern Spain. They were descendents of the oxen and cattle of ancient Asia and Europe. The black Andalusian bull was the bullfighter's foe in the bullrings of Spain. He was strong and fierce, with horns pointed forward to kill. On the American continents, these cattle bred quickly and their numbers grew. Many escaped capture and ran wild on the plains.

Another type of cattle was brought to Texas from Virginia, Georgia, and the Carolinas. After the American Revolution, some settlers from these areas decided to try their luck farther west. They traveled through the Louisiana Territory and settled in Texas. They brought with them Durham and Hereford cows that descended from stock originally brought from England. These cows were also inclined to break loose, and in Texas they mixed with the wild Spanish Andalusians to produce a new breed—the mighty Texas longhorn.

*Longhorns in a corral*

The Bettmann Archive

## GOOD COW SENSE

While they appeared to move as a wide river of cow flesh on cattle drives, cowboys knew that longhorns had distinct personalities. In order to move the herd, cowboys had to understand their cows. On the trail the strongest, most dominant steers would move to the front of the herd. The cowboys riding "point" focused on guiding these herd leaders along the desired path. With some careful and constant nudging by the cowboys, the rest of the herd calmly followed.

Texas longhorns grazed freely on the open range and multiplied quickly. Those that thrived were sturdy, long-legged, and thick-skinned. Their mighty horns measured five feet from tip to tip. Wild longhorns could travel for days without water. They lived in small groups hidden in the brush and ventured out only at night. They could swim across rivers and protect their calves from wolves.

Early Texas cowboys hunted these wild longhorns for their meat and hide. Later, they began gathering them into herds and branding them. They first began driving cattle out of Texas to New Orleans in the early 1840s and into California during the gold rush of 1849. A Texan's wealth wasn't measured by money, but by how many longhorns he owned.

*Mealtime during a roundup*

The famous cattle drives began in 1867 when cowboys drove cattle north to the new railroad lines in Kansas. These long, three-month drives over rough terrain could never have happened without the sturdy longhorn. The animals seldom got sick and could travel long distances between water holes. But they had a keen nose for the smell of water, and would sometimes stampede to the next water hole when thirsty. If things went smoothly on a drive, ten miles could be covered in a day.

Eventually, railroads were extended to all parts of the country and the cattle drives ended. Cows no longer had to survive the long, grueling days on the trail, so the tough stringy meat of the longhorn was replaced by more tender cow flesh. The Texas longhorn, like the old-time Texas cowboy, became a legend.

*Thirsty longhorns sometimes stampeded when they smelled water*

Before the drives were over, more than 5 million longhorns had been driven from Texas north to the Midwest. There is still a protected herd of longhorns in the Wichita Mountains Wildlife Refuge.

# The Cowtowns

Dodge City, Abilene, Wichita—these were the Kansas "cowtowns" where the trail met the railroad. Their names were magical to the cowboy because they meant the end of the long cattle drive. Trail work was non-stop, exhausting, and nerve-jangling. Cowboys worked grueling days and rode guard in shifts at night. For three months, their home was the range and their only company was other cowboys, horses, and cows. When they reached one of these cowtowns, they were ready to "raise a ruckus" and have some unbridled fun.

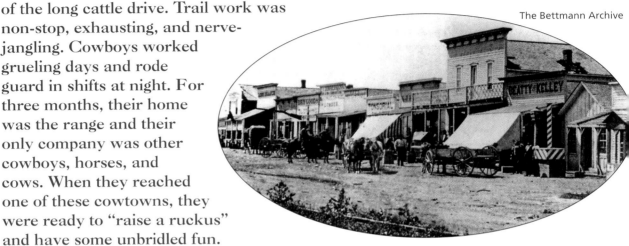

The Bettmann Archive

*Dodge City, Kansas, in 1878*

Abilene, Kansas, was the first cowtown. In 1867, cattleman Joe McCoy built a stockyard there next to the Union Pacific Railroad line. At that time, Abilene was a small frontier settlement. By winter, 35,000 cattle had reached Abilene from Texas by way of the Chisholm Trail. In 1872, the railroad reached Wichita, Kansas. By 1877, cowboys were driving longhorns up the Western Trail to Dodge City, Kansas, in the heart of buffalo country.

These towns became centers of western commerce, attracting more than just trail-weary cowboys. They were called "boom" towns because they grew so quickly, it seemed like they exploded.

Stores, hotels, saloons, real estate offices, banks, stables, and blacksmith shops appeared in what seemed like the blink of an eye. Gamblers, con artists, and thieves also arrived—looking for quick money. And they found it in the pockets of the cowboys. Three months on the trail earned a young cowboy about $75. Before he left town, he'd spent and gambled away almost all of it.

The first thing a cowboy off the trail did was get a haircut, a shave, a bath, and new clothes. Scrubbed and freshly dressed, the cowboy hit the streets, the saloons, dance halls, and gambling parlors.

*Playing cards at the town saloon*

## BOOT HILL

In the early days of Dodge City, Kansas, drunkenness and fighting were common. The fights often ended with a cowboy or gambler lying dead on the dirt street. These men had no relatives or friends to give them a proper burial. So the townsfolk carted them to the cemetery on the hill outside of town and buried them just as they were found on the street—still wearing their boots. The cemetery came to be called "Boot Hill."

Many of these cowboys were barely out of their teens. The cowtowns were their first taste of freedom and adulthood. In saloons like the Alamo, Applejack, and Lonestar, young cowboys quickly got dizzy drunk. Professional gamblers then went to work cheating them out of their hard-earned cash. In the early days of Abilene, as many as a thousand cowboys a night were out on the streets. By the late 1870s, Dodge City was called the "cowboy capital of the world."

*Rowdy cowboys ride through town*

The railroad divided Abilene right down the middle. On one side of the tracks were homes, the courthouse, and "townsfolk." On the other side were the stockyards, saloons, and gambling halls—the "Texas" side. To the proper townsfolk, the cowboy came from the wrong side of the tracks and was not a welcomed guest.

People of all kinds were moving west—homesteaders, gold seekers, railroad workers, veterans of the Civil War, and criminals fleeing the law. They all came together in the cowtowns. These towns were exciting and often dangerous places to be. Fights erupted easily. However, the typical cowboy quickly outgrew being rowdy. He made a point of leaving town with money in his pocket.

# The Cowboy's Workday

Ranchers kept some ranch hands on the payroll throughout the year. These were generally the older, more experienced cowboys. Until the 1880s, most ranch boundaries were not fenced. Cattle grazed in open pasture and often strayed onto other ranches. So cowboys worked as "line riders," patrolling the boundaries of the rancher's range.

Line riders lived in isolated camps, called "line shacks," along the ranch boundary. They rounded up stray cattle and drove them back toward the center of the ranch. They also guarded against rustlers and drove other ranchers' cows back toward their homes. Sometimes two line riders shared a line shack, but most line riders lived and worked alone. They often didn't see another human being for days or weeks at a time.

Other cowhands worked as "outriders" covering the entire range. In winter, they gathered and fed weak cattle and cut openings in ice-covered water holes. They rounded up cattle that had drifted in winter storms and drove them back to the ranch. Each rider had two horses for use in winter range riding. Some cowboys were kept busy feeding and tending the rancher's remuda during the winter months.

In early spring, "bog riders" pulled cows from mud

*Relaxing in the line shack*

bogs. Weakened cows were often knocked over and "bogged down" as cattle crowded muddy water holes.

The bog rider had to wade into the bog and pull the cow's legs from the mud. Then, on horseback, he roped the cow by the horns and pulled it out on its back. Bog riding was such hard work, riders often worked in pairs.

In spring, range riders also cleaned out clogged water holes. This was the season for gathering calves and pregnant cows that had been weakened by the winter. Spring roundup was held in May. Herds were sorted and calves branded. Ranchers hired full "outfits" of cowboys to cover the ranch districts and gather every cow.

In the Southwest during the summer months, blow-flies laid eggs in open wounds on cows. The cows became ill with screw worms. Range riders kept a lookout for sick cows and "doctored" their wounds.

In the fall, ranchers began putting together their remudas for the fall drives. Cowboys were hired to catch and break wild horses to the saddle. Calves born since the spring were branded. In late fall, calves were weaned from their mothers to give the cows a better chance of surviving the winter.

The nature of range work began to change

*Bogged down*

with the use of barbed wire fences and the closing of the open range. Line riders were no longer needed to patrol ranch boundaries. Fences now kept cattle from straying. To keep their jobs, unhappy cowboys were forced to climb down from their horses and become fence menders. They had to learn to use the new tools of the cowboy trade—wire cutters and pliers. They spent their time repairing fences damaged by cattle, rustlers, and winter storms. Line shacks were abandoned for bunkhouses, where ranch hands lived during the long, cold winters.

## BARBED WIRE FENCES

Before the 1870s ranchers could not fence in their herds. Wooden fences were far too expensive to build and maintain over large range areas. And cows would simply lean against plain wire fences until they collapsed. The invention of barbed wire changed the West forever. Cattle stayed clear of the sharp barbs twisted into the wire. Ranchers were able to fence off their lands, and the days of the group roundups were over.

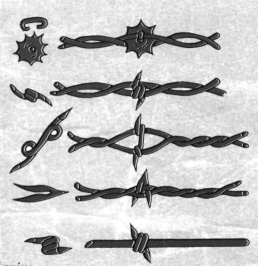

*Types of barbed wire*

# Law and Order

There were few judges and lawmen on the open range. So, just as the West offered a new chance to honest men and women, it offered many opportunities to the dishonest as well. When a criminal got away from the law in the East, people said he was "G.T.T."—Gone To Texas. Once on the wild plains of Texas, an outlaw could easily make his getaway on horseback to Mexico or move to a cowtown and take a new name.

On the cowboy's frontier, no man was as low and ornery as a horse thief. Since survival on the vast range depended on having a horse, stealing a man's horse was thought to be as evil as taking his life. And the penalty was death. If horses were stolen from a cattleman's remuda, a "vigilante" group was formed. Vigilantes took the law into their own hands. Cowboy vigilantes knew how to track horse thieves on the open range. And they knew how to tie a slipknot in a rope for a "necktie party"—a speedy hanging. Vigilantes acted quickly, without trials and legal judges. Often they hanged innocent men.

Next to the horse thief, the most hated man on the range was the cattle rustler. Rustlers were cowboys turned bad. They knew the cattle country and how to rope, ride, and brand. They used their skills to round up stray cattle and alter brands.

*An outlaw shoots a saloonkeeper*

## BILLY THE KID

One of the most famous outlaws of the Old West was Henry McCarty, better known as Billy the Kid. The "Kid" worked as a cowhand in New Mexico, and got involved with rustlers in a feud over grazing lands. Billy was arrested, but he escaped and formed a gang of cattle and horse thieves. Legend says he killed 21 men. Actually, he killed only three. Billy the Kid himself was finally killed at the age of 21 by Sheriff Pat Garrett in Lincoln County, New Mexico.

*Billy the Kid*

*Train robberies were common in the Wild West*

To deal with rustlers, ranchers would send their own cowhands after them. Cowboys had orders to "shoot first and ask questions later" when dealing with cattle rustlers.

Stagecoach and train robberies were frequent and costly. The famous Deadwood stage transported gold out of the Dakota Black Hills. It was held up so many times that it had to stop running. Cowtowns, too, were a favorite target of outlaw gangs because of all the money that was stored in the banks.

Tough law officers were hired to police the cowtowns. Some, like Wild Bill Hickok and Bat Masterson, became famous. Hickok had a reputation as a sharpshooter. Outlaws in Abilene generally stayed out of his way. Masterson served as sheriff of Dodge City for two years. He was quick on the draw and feared because of his dead aim. By the 1870s, many cattletowns had passed laws against carrying weapons in town. Cowboys were instructed to check their six-shooters at the livery stables with their horses.

The Texas Rangers were first formed in 1823 by the Spanish governor of Texas to protect settlers against Indian raids. After Texas gained independence from Mexico, a new group of Texas Rangers began policing the frontier. They guarded against horse and cattle thieves and later against fence cutters on the range. But the cattle frontier was too large for the Rangers alone to police. Vigilantes remained the main form of law and order in the Old West until the 1890s.

*The Dodge City Peace Commision, 1882*

The Bettmann Archive

# Cowboys and Indians

Long before the cowboy lassoed his first steer, Indians had lived for centuries on the Great Plains. These Native American hunters and farmers were the first people of the West. Several million Indians inhabited North America before the Europeans arrived. Tribal groups or bands moved across the deserts, plains, and mountains of the West, killing wild game as needed for food, clothing, and shelter. They lived in close relationship to their environment and never claimed to own it. They said it belonged to the Creator.

*An Indian village*

In 1540, when Coronado rode out of Mexico onto the Plains, he encountered Kiowa and Apache peoples. The Spanish conquistadors brought horses, cattle, guns, and the idea that humans could own land. Before long, the Plains Indians became superb horsemen hunting buffalo on horseback. But they still had very little contact with white men.

U.S. territory at the time of the Revolutionary War reached only to the Mississippi River. Then in 1803, the U.S. bought a vast area of land west of the Mississippi from France. This came to be known as the Louisiana Purchase. In 1804, President Thomas Jefferson sent the explorers Lewis and Clark across this territory to explore it. They were soon followed by increasing numbers of fur trappers and mountain men. Meanwhile, eastern Indians were driven west by government order. By the mid-1800s, a steady stream of settlers, gold miners, adventurers, and railroad men were sweeping over Indian lands. And on the Great Plains, cowboys began driving herds of cattle north from Texas through Indian country.

*Thomas Jefferson made the Louisiana Purchase in 1803*

In some ways, cowboys were much like Indians. Early cowboys didn't own land and had few possessions. Like Indians, they loved to ride, and felt at home on the wild plains. But as more and more cattle drives crossed native lands, cowboys and Indians came into conflict. Early drovers paid money and cattle to the Indians for permission to cross their territory.

## INDIAN HORSEMEN

One thing cowboys and Indians shared in common was their love of "horseflesh." The Indians' first horses came from the Spanish invaders and then from the growing wild herds. The horse made the Comanches the most powerful people of the central and southern plains. In the Northwest, Nez Percé Indians developed a special breed of "war pony" called the Appaloosa. Many cowboys had great respect for the Indians' ability to break and train horses without using force.

*Indians gently touched horses to tame them*

However, as cattle, homesteaders, miners, and railroads pushed across the West in larger numbers, the Indians were driven from their ancestral lands. The railroad divided the buffalo herds and scarred the land. White men wiped out the buffalo and the Native American way of life at the same time. On the Great Plains, cowboys on their long drives were caught in the middle of this struggle.

As Indians defended their lives and territories, the white settlers came to fear and hate the Indians. Comanches on the plains attacked white settlements. Apaches in west Texas raided herds and drove off cattle. Ranchers lost cows, horses, and sometimes their own lives. They formed armed groups to protect themselves against Indian raiders. The Texas Rangers also defended the cattle frontier against Indian attack.

After the Civil War, the U.S. government sent its army west to fight the Indians. The many bloody battles that followed are often called the "Indian Wars." By the 1870s, most of the Indians had been forced from their native lands and onto reservations by the U.S. Army.

*Comanche chief Quanah Parker*

# Famous Cowboys

**A**mong the thousands of cowboys who drove the long trails, only a few became famous. Some are remembered as trailblazers who opened the first cattle trails through Indian country. Others started as cowboys and later became open range ranchers. Cowboys who outgrew the trail sometimes found their way into politics or business. Some joined the early rodeos as the trail drives came to an end. Most were lost in the dust of history—their faces and names blurred with time. But some are remembered.

*Some cowboys wound up in politics*

In 1846, when he was nine years old, Charles Goodnight rode bareback from Illinois to Texas with his family. By the time he was 20, Goodnight was running cattle and building a herd of his own. After the Civil War, Goodnight had about 8,000 head of cattle but was losing them to Indian and Mexican rustlers. In 1866, he tried to drive 2,000 cows to New Mexico and Colorado, but they were stampeded and run off by Comanches. Later that year, he teamed up with the seasoned drover Oliver Loving for another drive through New Mexico.

Loving had driven the first herd of Texas longhorns to the Chicago market in 1858. His route became known as the Shawnee Trail.

## THE XIT RANCH

The famous XIT Ranch was 100 miles long, 27 miles wide, and covered 5 million acres of the Texas Panhandle. It took $7 million worth of barbed wire to fence the property in 1885. But the XIT never made much money. It wasn't owned by experienced cowboys or ranchers who knew the cattle business, but by four Chicago businessmen. In 1901, they began dividing and selling the ranch for farmland.

The Bettmann Archive

*Taking a break*

In 1860, he drove 1,000 head of cattle to the gold fields of Colorado, opening the Western Trail into Kansas. Loving had the experience and grit Goodnight needed to drive a herd through the stark Pecos country. During 1866, they made several profitable trips into New Mexico and opened the Goodnight-Loving Trail.

This trail snaked through rough, dry country, far from the protection of the Texas Rangers or the army. In 1867, Comanches began raids along the trail, driving off cattle and killing drovers. On one drive, Goodnight and Loving fought off a series of attacks but lost cattle and men. Goodnight took off to round up lost cattle, leaving Loving and a cowboy named One-Arm Wilson to drive the herd. The Comanches attacked Loving and Wilson on the Pecos. Loving died in New Mexico from wounds to his wrist and side.

Another cowboy trailblazer, Nelson Story, began his career as a shopkeeper and gold prospector in Montana. In 1866, he invested his gold in Texas longhorns and started the first long drive from Texas to Montana. His outfit encountered raiding Sioux in the Dakota badlands and held them off with Remington rifles. The drive took five months and covered 2,500 miles. Story was the first to bring the longhorn and the cowboy to the northern ranges.

*Charles Goodnight invented the chuck wagon*

John Chisum was another Texas cowboy with big ideas. Born in Tennessee, Chisum moved to Texas when he was a boy. By the 1850s, he was busy helping himself to stray cattle and building a herd. In 1867, he began herding cattle west into New Mexico and was soon selling 10,000 head a year. At the time of his death in 1884, Chisum's cattle empire stretched from Pecos, Texas, to Roswell, New Mexico. He employed 100 cowboys who branded 18,000 calves a year on his El Rancho Grande.

# The Working Cowgirl

There were no "cowgirls" on the payrolls of the long drives north. In the 1860s, '70s, and '80s, women didn't do the work of cowboys—or did they? The truth is that some did. Old ranch records don't list women as paid cowhands. But daughters, sisters, and ranchers' wives often rode, roped calves, and "punched cows"—as herding livestock was often called—alongside their fathers, brothers, and husbands. Sometimes they were paid off the record, or not at all. Still, they did the work of cowboys and bit the same range dust.

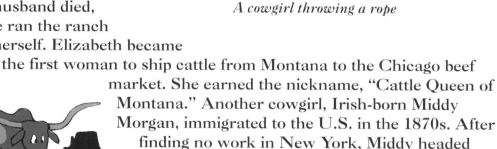

*A cowgirl throwing a rope*

In the 1880s, Elizabeth Collins went into the cattle business with her husband in Montana. After her husband died, she ran the ranch herself. Elizabeth became the first woman to ship cattle from Montana to the Chicago beef market. She earned the nickname, "Cattle Queen of Montana." Another cowgirl, Irish-born Middy Morgan, immigrated to the U.S. in the 1870s. After finding no work in New York, Middy headed west and was hired as a ranch hand in Montana. She was so good at working cattle that she became a partner in the ranch. She achieved an international reputation for her knowledge of breeding and raising cattle.

Agnes Morley Cleaveland grew up in the 1880s and '90s working a ranch with her mother and brother. For comfort and convenience when riding, she gave up her sunbonnet, dress, and sidesaddle for a "five gallon" hat, flannel shirt, and blue denim knickers and skirt.

*Heating up a brand*

## ALICE AND MARGE GREENOUGH, BRONC BUSTERS

In the 1920s and '30s, Alice Greenough and her sister Marge were two of the best women bronc riders on the rodeo circuit. They were born on a homestead near Red Lodge, Montana. In the early 1920s, they began competing in relay races and bronc riding exhibitions. They joined King's Wild West Show and began touring the country. By 1940, the Greenough sisters were among the best known rodeo performers in the world.

Women like Agnes Cleaveland wrote about their lives and times. But many more whose names are lost and forgotten also ran cattle and horses from the saddle. Other girls growing up on Great Plains homesteads and Texas ranches learned to "ride before they could walk." Some of these women drifted into the early rodeos like Buffalo Bill's Wild West Show of the 1880s. Mrs. Georgie Duffy was billed as the "Rough Rider from Wyoming."

During the 1920s and '30s, women like Tad Lucas and Prairie Rose Henderson became professional rodeo entertainers. Women competed against other women in skills like bronc riding, trick riding, and racing. Fox Hastings was a noted woman "bull-dogger" and steer "rastler" in the 1920s. In 1948, the first all-girls rodeo was held in Amarillo, Texas. Today, the Professional Women's Rodeo Association has more than 2,000 members.

In every ranch county of today's West, women are working as cowgirls or ranch hands. They work the roundups, break horses, and ride fence along with their cowboy fathers, brothers, and co-workers. Some of these women were reared on ranches and others worked their way in from the outside. Some work alongside their husbands. Others own their own ranches, or work as hired hands. All face some discrimination because they are women in a traditional "man's job." But over the past 125 years, women have proven their worth as working cowgirls.

*TEXAS HIGHWAYS Magazine/TxDOT*

*A cowgirl posing with her guns*

# Black Cowboys of the West

Cowboys came in more colors than one. In fact, some of the first cowboys in the Americas were Africans. Africans sailed with Columbus and accompanied Cortés into Mexico. In Venezuela, Argentina, and Mexico, African slaves hunted and herded Spanish cattle. Later, in North American slave states, black slaves tended their owners' cattle.

Slave holders migrated into Texas in the early 1800s, taking their slaves with them. By 1860, there were 180,000 African American slaves in Texas. Many were skilled horsemen, roping and branding cattle on the open range. After the Civil War, many freed slaves drifted west. But African American frontier families did not find racial equality among whites.

The black cowboy, however, found work at an equal wage. And on the open range of the Great Plains, former slaves who became cowboys felt a new freedom. They embraced the land and the cowboy life.

A quarter of the cowboys who drove cattle on the Chisholm and Western trails were black men. During the years of the big drives, 5,000 black cowboys "headed 'em north." With nicknames like "Deadwood Dick" and "Arizona Joe," black cowboys sometimes achieved fame.

The Bettmann Archive

*Black and white cowboys worked together on the open range*

Nat Love was one of many cowboys called by the name "Deadwood Dick." In his memoirs, Love writes that he earned the name after winning a roping contest in Deadwood, Arizona. He was born a slave in Tennessee around 1854 and drifted to Ohio and Kansas after the Civil War. In Dodge City, he hired onto a cowboy outfit at $30 a month and began his career punching cows. By his own recollection, Love was a hero—a fearless, two-fisted superman on horseback. He claimed he was shot 14 times, but the bullets couldn't kill him. Like many cowboy storytellers, "Deadwood Dick" could stretch the truth pretty thin.

*Nat Love*

Bob Lott, Jim Taylor, and Arthur L. Walker were just a few of the other black cowboys who worked the open range. They didn't all achieve the fame of Nat Love, but they did their share of cow-punching.

One black cowboy who earned success in Texas was "80 John" Wallace. 80 John was born into slavery and became a working cowboy at the age of 15. Later, he became one of the first African American ranchers in Texas.

Despite these triumphs, black cowboys faced racial prejudice. Though they earned the same wage as white cowboys, they didn't get promoted as often. Blacks seldom became trail bosses or foremen. They were often given low-status jobs as horse wranglers or danger- ous jobs as bronco busters. And they faced discrimination in frontier towns. Some saloons segregated black cowboys at one end of the bar. But they shared meals, horses, and campfires freely on the trail with other cowboys. On the open range, a cowboy's talents usually mattered more than his skin color.

### BULLDOGGING THE BULL

Bill Pickett was a black cowboy who became famous for fancy "steer rastling." Pickett worked the 101 Ranch in Oklahoma where he claimed he invented the rodeo sport of "bulldogging." A bulldogger rides after a steer, jumps off his horse, and wrestles the steer to the ground by the horns. Pickett died in 1932 at the age of 71 after a horse kicked him in the head. But he died on his own 160-acre ranch in Oklahoma.

*Bill Pickett*

# The Vaquero

The Mexican vaqueros were the first cowboys of the American Southwest. They were usually mestizos, people of mixed Spanish and native South American blood. Their ancestors were the first wild cattle hunters on the plains of South America. In the 1700s, vaqueros migrated from Mexico with Spanish Catholic missionaries to California and Texas. Both were then owned by Mexico. The missionaries tried to convert Indians to Christianity while the vaqueros tended mission cattle herds. The vaqueros also trained Indians in herding and horsemanship. Wearing short jackets, *serape* (say-RAH-pay) shawls, and sombreros, the vaqueros rode the Texas plains.

In the early 1800s, when Texas still belonged to Mexico, the Texas vaquero introduced settlers from the United States, called Anglos, to the skills and craft of the western cowboy. The vaquero made his own saddle from rawhide. He also braided his own *la reata*, or rope lariat, from rawhide strips. He made a loop on one end to lasso cows and horses. When roping a cow, he'd wrap his lariat around the saddle horn to secure his hold.

*Vaqueros watching bulls fight*

## THE CALIFORNIOS

Mexican vaqueros migrated into California with the first Spanish missions in 1769. They drove cattle up the coast onto rich California grazing lands. Vaqueros worked the mission herds of wealthy ranchers. These vaqueros were the first Spanish Californians, or *Californios.* As the herds grew, vaqueros trained California Indians to ride and tend cattle. In 1832, California vaqueros were recruited to teach native Hawaiians the tools of the cowboy trade.

*A Spanish mission in California*

The Anglo Texas cowboys learned this roping style from the vaquero. Anglos called it "dallying," from the vaquero expression, *da la vuelta*, or "give the turn."

The vaquero made his own *chaparejos* to protect his legs when riding through tall brush. The Anglo Texas cowboy used these leggings too, calling them "chaps." On the southern plains of Texas, chaps protected against prickly pear and tall mesquite.

Early vaqueros in Texas didn't carry guns. The vaquero's only weapon was his knife, which he could throw with deadly accuracy. Knives were also useful tools for working leather.

In rainstorms and on cold nights, the vaquero rode wrapped in his serape, or shawl. When bedding down, it served as his bedroll. Colors and weaves of the vaquero's serape were influenced by his Indian and Spanish heritage.

*A vaquero in traditional dress*

The vaquero who later rode with Texas cowboys on trail drives north was not treated as an equal. He earned half the wages of Anglo cowboys, though he did the same work. He was seldom promoted to trail boss, though his skills as horseman and roper were well known. The vaquero was rejected, in part, because he was Mexican. Texas had gained independence from Mexico in a bloody war. The vaquero had been an enemy. In Latin America too, vaqueros were regarded as inferior by Spanish ranchers called *caballeros* (cah-bah-YAY-rose). Racial prejudice against "half-breeds," Native Americans, and blacks was widespread throughout the Americas.

Despite this bigotry, the Mexican American cowboy made his mark on cowboy culture in the West. In the 1870s, a vaquero named Juan Redon was foreman on the largest ranch in Oregon. At the turn of the century, half the cowboys working on northwestern ranches were Mexican American. The vaquero, a laborer on horseback, left his brand on cowboy history.

# The Rodeo Trail

The rodeo has its roots in the Mexican *rodeo* (roh-DAY-oh), or roundup. As early as the 1550s, vaqueros in Mexico were rounding up wild cattle and branding calves. When the roundup work was done, the vaqueros took time to "horse around." They competed in various riding contests and tested their skills in handling cattle.

Throughout the Americas, cowboys had similar competitions. Huasos in Chile raced on horseback and skid their horses to a sit-down stop. Argentine gauchos competed in riding wild steers and in "tailing" or grabbing a bull by the tail and tumbling it to the ground. Vaqueros played a rowdy game of tag on horseback called *juego de la vara* (HWAY-goh day la VAH-rah), or the "rod game," which is similar to the children's game "duck, duck, goose." Most of these rodeo games and contests tested a cowboy's work skills—riding, roping, and punching cattle.

The vaquero brought his love of work and play on horseback to the American Southwest. Competition between ranches became a part of the Texas roundup. After herds were separated and calves branded, the old-time cowboys matched skills in contests like steer roping, horse racing, bulldogging, and bronc riding.

*Chief Sitting Bull and Buffalo Bill Cody, around 1880*

The Bettmann Archive

In time, these contests became a popular form of entertainment on the western frontier. Cowboys competed in public exhibitions at Independence Day celebrations in Colorado, Wyoming, and Texas. One of the first public rodeos was held in Prescott, Arizona, in 1864. Towns staged rodeos to promote business. In 1910 in Pendleton, Oregon, a public "roundup" was held with "buffalo bucking," Indian dances, and a wild horse race.

In 1883, Buffalo Bill Cody took his Wild West Show on the road. Unlike the first Mexican rodeos and Texas roundups, the Wild West Shows were "cowboy and Indian circuses." There were demonstrations of sharpshooting and roping, and re-creations of stagecoach robberies and Indian fights. A cowgirl called Little Annie Oakley entertained crowds with her sharpshooting.

Wild West shows made heroes of the western cowboy and cowgirl in eastern cities as well as in the big cities of Europe. They had nothing to do with actual roundups and cattle drives, however. By 1931, the last of the great Wild West Shows, the Millers Brothers Show, had folded. But rodeo shows continued to grow.

Early rodeo cowboys, like the bulldogger Bill Pickett, had learned their skills on the job. Pickett developed his style of steer wrestling after watching a bulldog work cattle on a Texas ranch. In time, rodeo performers were no longer working cowboys, but professional competitors. The Cowboy's Turtle Association was formed in 1936 as a union of rodeo professionals. No one is certain where the name came from, but their motto was "slow but sure." Since 1974, it's been called the Professional Rodeo Cowboys Association. The rodeo of today is a show for cowboy athletes to demonstrate their skills and training.

*Annie Oakley taking aim*

## THE RING RACE AND JOUSTING

Some of the earliest rodeo contests were brought to the Americas by Spanish horsemen. *La sortija* (lah sor-TEE-hah), or the "ring race," became part of the cowboy tradition in Chile and Argentina. A galloping rider holding a foot-long lance tried to drive it through the center of a small ring that dangled on a string. In *juego de canas* (HWAY-goh day CAH-nahs), or "jousting with canes," galloping horsemen threw cane lances at each other. They got points for hitting their opponents and for catching lances thrown at them.

*La sortija*

# Cowboy Songs and Poetry

Old-time cowboys didn't sit around the campfire strumming guitars. Guitars were too big and fragile to take on the long drive. But some cowboys did pack small instruments like harmonicas and jew's harps. A lilting melody or two pierced the night air before an outfit collapsed into sleep. Off in the distance, night riders circled the herd in shifts, keeping watch on a couple thousand bedded-down cows. And while he rode guard, the night rider often sang or hummed to the sleeping cattle. Somehow his voice reassured the cows and kept them from being spooked by noises in the night.

In those solitary moments, night riders sang or recited almost anything that came to mind—an old lullaby, a passage from the Bible, even labels memorized from canned foods. The lyrics didn't matter much to the cows. Cowboys often made up new words to old melodies, words that told about their own lives. Some songs were picked up by other cowboys, who added their own words. That's how songs like "Texas Cowboy" were born.

*Cowboys often sang to the cows at night to calm them*

> *Oh, I am a Texas cowboy, right off the Texas plains,*
> *My trade is cinching saddles, and pulling of bridle reins.*
> *And I can throw a lasso with the greatest of ease,*
> *I can rope and ride a bronco any way I please.*

Life on the plains required the cowboy to be tough, but he could also be tender. Sometimes the cowboy expressed his affection for the herd in a song like "Git Along Little Dogies." "Dogies" were motherless calves.

> *As I was a-walking one morning for pleasure,*
> *I spied a young cow puncher riding alone.*
> *His hat was throwed back and his spurs was a-jingling,*
> *As he approached me a-singing this song.*

*"Whoopee ti yi yo, git along little dogies,*
*It's your misfortune and none of my own.*
*Whoopee ti yi yo, git along little dogies,*
*For you know Wyoming will be your new home."*

The cowboy sang of work, adventure, loneliness, and hard luck. The well known ballad, "The Cowboy's Lament," tells the tale of a dying cowboy.

*As I rode down to the streets of Laredo,*
*As I rode down to Laredo one day,*
*I saw a young cowboy all dressed in white linen,*
*All dressed in white linen, and cold as the clay.*

*"I see by your outfit that you are a cowboy,"*
*These words he spoke as I went strolling by.*
*"Come sit here beside me and hear my sad story,*
*For I'm shot through the body and know I must die.*

*So play the fife slowly and beat the drum lowly,*
*And play the death march as you bear me along,*
*Just take me to Boot Hill and chuck the sod o'er me,*
*For I'm a poor cowboy and I know I've done wrong."*

Cowboys didn't necessarily sing well. But their words and songs were genuine—and from the heart.

## ROUNDUP RHYMES

At roundups, hundreds of cowboys came together to separate herds. They gathered over several days, and the first to arrive passed the time swapping stories, jokes, and songs. They performed songs and poems—often humorous—that they had composed in the saddle, like this one:

*Storytelling on a starry night*

*I was punching down on Boggy Creek where the quicksand got so bad,*
*One-eyed Sam with a lasso in hand roped me over my head,*
*He pulled and yanked as I almost sank and sand ran with my tears,*
*But he choked me good 'til on ground I stood, and the sand run out my ears.*

# The Range Wars

The old-time cowboy rode an unfenced open range, where cattle often strayed from their herds. The first Texas cattlemen built their herds from these stray cattle, called "mavericks." Any unbranded cow or calf was considered free for the taking. Mexicans and Texans regularly rustled cattle from each other's herds, and Indians rustled from both.

By the 1880s, however, large ranches were being fenced with barbed wire. Big-time ranchers began forming cattlemen's associations to prevent mavericking and to guard the best grasslands and water. Cowboys found it harder to build their own herds. Small-time ranchers were fenced off of grazing lands and water holes by the cattlemen. To make matters worse, wealthy ranchers often fenced off public lands and claimed them as private property. Trouble was brewing.

The Bettmann Archive

Throughout cattle country, small-time ranchers and cowboys became "fence-cutters." They formed secret groups with names like the "Owls" and "Javelines" to take down fences and bring back the open range. In 1883, a drought hit Texas and water holes became scarce. Desperate small-time cattlemen and cowboys cut fences to get at any available water. Wealthy cattlemen hired armed guards to stop them. Many small cattlemen were taken out and hanged as "cattle rustlers" by these hired guards.

*Masked cattlemen fire on a sheepherder's flock*

## THE JOHNSON COUNTY WAR

In the late 1800s, when the open range on the central and southern plains began to be fenced, cattlemen drove thousands of cattle to the grasslands of Montana and Wyoming, the last open range. Conflict followed close behind. In Wyoming in 1892, a group of small-time ranchers and homesteading farmers challenged the cattle kings. Many of them stole cattle from the big ranchers. They elected themselves to most of the public offices, including positions as judges. Seldom would these judges of Johnson County convict a rustler. So the wealthy cattlemen put together an army of vigilantes, many of them dishonest men brought in from Texas, to attack the small operators. The fighting that broke out came to be called the Johnson County War.

On the Great Plains, the Old West of the cattle kings was changing. Homesteaders and sheepherders began to arrive from the East to build farms. They were not welcomed by the cattlemen. Ranchers believed that sheep chewed grasses down to the root and polluted the watering holes. Homesteaders usually settled near the best watering holes and put up fences to keep their livestock in. The fences also kept the range cattle out. Cattlemen declared that the West was a cattle kingdom and that it wasn't big enough for both cattle and sheep.

*A sheep farm in the West, 1887*

So cattlemen began organizing attacks on sheepherders, their flocks, and on homesteading farmers. They would ride under cover of night to slaughter entire flocks of sheep, slitting their throats or clubbing them to death. They burned homesteaders' houses and knocked down their fences. In 1894 in Garfield County, Colorado, cattlemen stampeded 3,800 sheep over a bluff into Parachute Creek below. Flocks were dynamited and poisoned, and sheepherders were killed in their sleep.

These range wars continued into this century, but the fences stayed up. The federal government had given the railroads large strips of land to pay for building tracks across the West. In the late 1800s, the railroads began selling much of this land to homesteaders from the east and to immigrants from Europe. The railroads had first caused the Great Plains to become cattle country. Then, they turned cattle country into farm lands. In the end, the open range of the Old West was divided by fences.

*Homesteaders building a fence*

# Cattle and the Environment

The early herds of wild cows on the Great Plains shared grazing lands and water holes with other wild animals. In time, however, larger areas of open range were overrun with cattle as cowboys and cattlemen increased their herds. Once cattle ranching became big business, western lands were changed forever.

Change began in 1867 with the first Texas cattle drives to railroad depots in Kansas. At that time, millions of wild buffalo still roamed the Plains. Native peoples such as the Lakota and the Cheyenne thrived in the wilderness. They hunted buffalo and other animals for their meat, hides, and bones, taking only what they needed to survive.

Native plants, shrubs, and grasses swept the Great Plains from Texas to Montana. Wild buffalo grass and bluestem bunch grasses kept soil from being eroded, or worn away, by wind and rain. Plains animals such as elk, bobcats, and birds found water and shelter along Plains rivers and streams. The Great Plains was a balanced ecosystem, a web of relationships among living things. All this changed when longhorn cattle began tramping out of Texas.

Each beef cow on the long drive ate 900 pounds of grass and shrubs in a month. Cowboys drove hundreds of thousands of "beeves" each year to the railroads and northern ranges. Indians who were in the path of the cattle drives were driven out or killed.

*Cattle beat the ground bare with their powerful hooves*

## RANCHING AND THE FUTURE

Cowboys and cattle have made a great contribution to the growth of our country. Many people, however, believe that excessive cattle raising is harming the world. Today, cattle, sheep, and other livestock are fed 70 percent of the grains grown in the U.S. while many people go hungry. Some say our western grasslands continue to be overgrazed. All over the world, native peoples, trees, and animals are being destroyed to make room for more cattle ranches. Lands and vegetation that once fed people now feed cows. We need to ask ourselves, "What's best for tomorrow?"

*Millions of buffalo were killed off in the 1860s and '70s*

Cattlemen, railroad builders, and the U.S. Army fought to open the Plains to ranching and white settlers. Cowboys claimed that buffalo were a menace to the long drive, causing cattle to stampede. Buffalo herds were slaughtered with rifles to make room for more cattle and railroads.

Indians defended their villages and hunting grounds against the invading railroaders, cattlemen, and settlers. But by the late 1870s, the buffalo were almost extinct. Plains tribes lost their food source, their native lands, and many lives. The Great Plains had become "cattle country."

Grasslands, streams, and ponds were overrun with beef cows. They over-grazed the land, eating almost all of the native bunchgrasses. Other grasses, such as one called "cheat grass," took their place. But cheat grass burns easily in the hot sun and is not as nutritious for animals as the native grasses.

Cattle also trampled the grasslands. Their powerful hooves beat the ground bare. In time, topsoil was eroded by wind and rain. Lush grasslands became deserts. The wild animals that lived there died off or fled.

Almost 500 years have passed since Spanish cows entered the Great Plains. The great buffalo herds that once roamed the grasslands are no more. The once wild hunting grounds of Plains Indians are now farms and ranches. But cows and cattle business continue to shape western lands.

*The Bettmann Archive*

*A pile of 40,000 buffalo hides in Dodge City, Kansas, 1878*

# The Cowboy of Today

More than one hundred years after the last of the great cattle drives, the cowboy still rides. He still punches cows on horseback from Texas to Oregon, ropes and brands, and rounds up cattle.

There are million-acre ranches in Nevada and Montana. Great Plains grasses still nourish semi-wild cattle and small herds of wild mustangs. The buffalo is gone from the Plains, however, and so are the days of three-month cattle drives over wild frontier. There is no longer a need to drive cattle over long distances. Railroads reach every part of the country, so a rancher needs only to load his cows into the nearest cattle car.

The cowboy adjusted to changing times. He learned to live with barbed wire fences, and he learned to repair gasoline engines. Some have learned to herd cows with sheep dogs while others use helicopters and all-terrain vehicles. But the typical cowboy still does most of his work from his "rig," as he sometimes calls his saddle. He can still cut a single steer from a herd or circle the herd to stop a stampede.

The working cowboy of today is called a buckaroo in the Northwest, a vaquero in California and Mexico, and a brush hand in south Texas. What makes him a cowboy is his work. He knows the nature and instinct of cattle.

The Bettmann Archive

*The roundup of today looks much like it did a hundred years ago*

He knows the herd and how it behaves. Like the old-time cowboy, he has the skills of a blacksmith, harness maker, and "cow doctor." He can "bust a bronc," brand cows, and birth calves like his great-grandfather did. And he's just as handy with a rope. But he also knows how to use a tractor and hay baler. He can repair a water pump and irrigate a field. He can repair a pickup truck and herd cattle with it, but he still prefers a mustang to a Chevy.

*A horse trailer is a part of the modern cowboy's gear*

Although the open range is gone, the modern cowboy may still work ranches that are 50 miles long and wide. Roundups today look pretty much like they did 100 years ago. There's the same dust and rush of cattle, bawling of calves, and sizzle of the branding iron. The chuckwagon is still there, even if it has rubber tires. The grub is about the same— canned vegetables, bacon, beans, fresh-cooked biscuits. But the cowboy has also learned the art of herding steers into a truck trailer and "running" wild horses with a helicopter.

Some cowboys today still don't like to be tied down to one job. They hire onto an outfit for days or weeks, pull their pay, then beat a trail to the next ranch. Others work at building their own herds and save to buy their own land. Some cowhands today are cowgirls, roping and riding, training horses, and running steers.

*Some modern cowboys use helicopters to herd cattle*

43

*A cattle ranch in Colorado*

The cowboy's clothes—chaps, hat, boots, and spurs—haven't changed much either. Fewer cowboys today make their own garments and equipment, but some still do. The cowboy crafts of braiding rawhide and hair ropes into lariats, reins, and headstalls are still practiced today.

Regional cowboy traditions and styles have continued over the past 100 years. In California, the pace of work is still slower and more relaxed. Vaqueros still don't use bit bridles like cowboys east of the Rockies do. They prefer the old hackamore halters of their ancestors. The Montana cowboy still creases his high hat at the front. But no matter the differences among cowboys, all of them are part of an American legend known around the world.

## MODERN COWBOY GEAR

Some of the modern cowboy's gear is easy to identify, like the tractor and pickup truck. But there have been other changes in cowboy equipment as well. Fence riders today carry their pliers and staples in a special leather pocket tied to a saddle string. Modern horse hoods with goggles protect a horse's eyes while the animal is transported in a trailer. And reinforced canvas saddle bags are used by rodeo riders to protect their saddles when on the road between shows.

# INDEX

## EXTREMELY WEIRD SERIES

*A*ll of the titles are written by Sarah Lovett, 8½" x 11", 48 pages, $9.95 paperbacks, with color photographs and illustrations

Extremely Weird Bats
Extremely Weird Birds
Extremely Weird Endangered Species
Extremely Weird Fishes
Extremely Weird Frogs
Extremely Weird Insects
Extremely Weird Mammals
Extremely Weird Micro Monsters
Extremely Weird Primates
Extremely Weird Reptiles
Extremely Weird Sea Creatures
Extremely Weird Snakes
Extremely Weird Spiders

## X-RAY VISION SERIES

*E*ach title in the series is 8½" x 11", 48 pages, $9.95 paperback, with color photographs and illustrations, and written by Ron Schultz.

Looking Inside the Brain
Looking Inside Cartoon Animation
Looking Inside Caves and Caverns
Looking Inside Sports Aerodynamics
Looking Inside Sunken Treasure
Looking Inside Telescopes and the Night Sky

## THE KIDDING AROUND TRAVEL GUIDES

*A*ll of the titles listed below are 64 pages and $9.95 paperbacks, except for *Kidding Around the National Parks* and *Kidding Around Spain*, which are 108 pages and $12.95 paperbacks.

Kidding Around Atlanta
Kidding Around Boston, 2nd ed.
Kidding Around Chicago, 2nd ed.
Kidding Around the Hawaiian Islands
Kidding Around London
Kidding Around Los Angeles
Kidding Around the National Parks
  of the Southwest
Kidding Around New York City, 2nd ed.
Kidding Around Paris
Kidding Around Philadelphia
Kidding Around San Diego
Kidding Around San Francisco
Kidding Around Santa Fe
Kidding Around Seattle
Kidding Around Spain
Kidding Around Washington, D.C., 2nd ed.

## MASTERS OF MOTION SERIES

*E*ach title in the series is 10¼" x 9", 48 pages, $9.95 paperback, with color photographs and illustrations.

**How to Drive an Indy Race Car**
  David Rubel
**How to Fly a 747**
  Tim Paulson
**How to Fly the Space Shuttle**
  Russell Shorto

## THE KIDS EXPLORE SERIES

*E*ach title is written by kids for kids by the Westridge Young Writers Workshop, 7" x 9", and $9.95 paperback, with photographs and illustrations by the kids.

**Kids Explore America's Hispanic Heritage**
112 pages
**Kids Explore America's African American Heritage** 128 pages
**Kids Explore the Gifts of Children with Special Needs** 128 pages
**Kids Explore America's Japanese American Heritage** 144 pages

## ENVIRONMENTAL TITLES

**Habitats:** *Where the Wild Things Live*
Randi Hacker and Jackie Kaufman
8½" x 11", 48 pages, color illustrations, $9.95 paper

**The Indian Way:** *Learning to Communicate with Mother Earth*
Gary McLain
7" x 9", 114 pages, two-color illustrations, $9.95 paper

**Rads, Ergs, and Cheeseburgers:** *The Kids' Guide to Energy and the Environment*
Bill Yanda
7" x 9", 108 pages, two-color illustrations, $13.95 paper

**The Kids' Environment Book:** *What's Awry and Why*
Anne Pedersen
7" x 9", 192 pages, two-color illustrations, $13.95 paper

## BIZARRE & BEAUTIFUL SERIES

*A* spirited and fun investigation of the mysteries of the five senses in the animal kingdom.

Each title in the series is 8½" x 11", $14.95 hardcover, with color photographs and illustrations throughout.

**Bizarre & Beautiful Ears**
**Bizarre & Beautiful Eyes**
**Bizarre & Beautiful Feelers**
**Bizarre & Beautiful Noses**
**Bizarre & Beautiful Tongues**

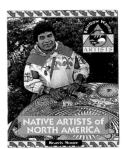 

## RAINBOW WARRIOR SERIES

*W* hat is a Rainbow Warrior Artist? It is a person who strives to live in harmony with the Earth and all living creatures, and who tries to better the world while livi his or her life in a creative way.

Each title is written by Reavis Moore with a foreword by LeVa Burton, and is 8½" x 11", 48 pages, $14.95 hardcover, with color photographs and illustrations.

**Native Artists of Africa**
**Native Artists of North America**
**Native Artists of Europe (available 9/94)**

## ROUGH AND READY SERIES

*L* earn about the men and women who settled the American West. Explore the myths and legends about these courageous individuals and learn about the environmental, cultural, and economic legacies they left to us.

Each title in the series is written by A. S. Gintzler and is 48 pages, 8½" x 11", $12.95 hardcover, with two-color illustrations and duotone archival photographs.

Available 7/94:

**Rough and Ready Cowboys**
**Rough and Ready Homesteaders**
**Rough and Ready Prospectors**

**Rough and Ready Loggers**
**Rough and Ready Outlaws & Lawmen**
**Rough and Ready Railroaders**

## AMERICAN ORIGINS SERIES

*M* any of us are the third and fourth generation of our families to live in America. Learn what our great-gr grandparents experienced when they arrived here a how much of our lives are still intertwined with theirs.

Each title is 48 pages, 8½" x 11", $12.95 hardcover, with two-color illustrations and duotone archival photographs.

Available 6/94:

**Tracing Our German Roots**
**Tracing Our Irish Roots**
**Tracing Our Italian Roots**
**Tracing Our Jewish Roots**

**Tracing Our Chinese Roots**
**Tracing Our Japanese Roots**
**Tracing Our Polish Roots**

**ORDERING INFORMATION**
Please check your local bookstore for our books, or call 1-800-888-7504 to order direct from us. All orders are shipped via UPS; see chart below to calculate your shipping charge for U.S. destinations. **No P.O. Boxes please; we must have a street address to ensure delivery.** If the book you request is not available, we will hold your check until we can ship it. Foreign orders will be shipped surface rate unless otherwise requested; please enclose $3.00 for the first item and $1.00 for each additional item.

**METHOD OF PAYMENT**
Check, money order, American Express, MasterCard, or VISA. We cannot be responsible for cash sent through the mail. For credit card orders, include your card number, expiration date, and your signature, or call 1-800-888-7504. American Express card orders can be shipped only to billing address of card holder. Sorry, no C.O.D.'s. Residents of sunny New Mexico, add 6.25% tax to total.

Address all orders and inquiries to:   John Muir Publications
P.O. Box 613
Santa Fe, NM 87504

(505) 982-4078
**(800) 888-7504**

| For U.S. Orders Totaling | Add |
|---|---|
| Up to $15.00 | $4.25 |
| $15.01 to $45.00 | $5.25 |
| $45.01 to $75.00 | $6.25 |
| $75.01 or more | $7.25 |